Table Of Contents

Interduction

"Crowd" is a captivating novel that explores the theme of isolation in a world that is increasingly interconnected. Written by the acclaimed author, Prince of Peace, the book is a must-read for anyone who has ever felt disconnected from the world around them.

Set in the not-too-distant future, "Crowd" tells the story of a society where people have become so absorbed in their digital lives that they have lost touch with the real world. The protagonist, a young woman named Lin, is struggling to find her place in this society. She feels like an outsider and is desperate for a sense of connection and belonging.

As Lin navigates her way through this isolated world, she discovers an underground movement of people who are also searching for a deeper connection. Together, they embark on a journey of self-discovery and self-acceptance that challenges the status quo and forces them to confront their own fears and limitations.

What makes "Crowd" such a compelling read is the way it captures the complexities of modern life. Prince of Peace writing is both insightful and thought-provoking, and his characters are relatable and engaging. The novel is a powerful reminder of the importance of human connection and the dangers of living in a world where technology has replaced genuine human interaction.

In short, "Crowd" is a beautifully written and deeply moving novel that deserves to be on everyone's reading list. It is a powerful meditation on the human condition and a must-read for anyone who has ever felt alone in a crowded world.

Chapter 1: The Invitation

An Unexpected Party

As the main character in "Alone in a Crowd: A Novel of Isolation" reflects on the events leading up to the unexpected party, feelings of betrayal and abandonment come to the surface. The title of the subchapter, "An Unexpected Party," sets the stage for a turning point in the protagonist's journey towards self-discovery and acceptance.

In this pivotal scene, the protagonist is confronted with the harsh reality of being alone in a crowd of people who were once thought to be friends. The party serves as a stark reminder of the isolation and disconnect that has plagued the protagonist's life, despite efforts to reach out and connect with others.

The subchapter delves into the protagonist's internal struggles and conflicting emotions as they navigate the unfamiliar terrain of social interactions and expectations. The title, "An Unexpected Party," hints at the unexpected twists and turns that life can take, leaving the protagonist feeling lost and adrift in a sea of faces.

For the audience of "I thought you would have been there for me," this subchapter serves as a poignant reminder of the complexities of human relationships and the impact of feeling isolated and misunderstood. The niches of "I Can't Do This All by My Self: A Novel" resonate with the struggles and challenges faced by the protagonist, as they grapple with their own sense of self-worth and belonging.

Ultimately, "An Unexpected Party" offers a glimpse into the protagonist's internal world and the journey towards finding solace and acceptance in the face of isolation. The subchapter serves as a powerful exploration of the human experience and the universal longing for connection and understanding. Feeling Out of Place

In the subchapter "Feeling Out of Place" from the novel "Alone in a Crowd: A Novel of Isolation," the protagonist grapples with the overwhelming sense of being disconnected from those around them. The feeling of being out of place, of not belonging, weighs heavily on their shoulders as they navigate the complexities of relationships and social interactions.

Addressed to an audience of "I thought you would have been there for me," the subchapter delves into the disappointment and confusion that can arise when expectations are not met. The protagonist reflects on their vulnerability and the deep desire for support and understanding from those they care about. The pain of feeling alone in a crowd, of not being seen or heard, resonates throughout the narrative.

As the story unfolds, the protagonist grapples with the harsh reality that they cannot do it all by themselves. The isolation and loneliness they experience serve as a stark reminder of the importance of connection and belonging. The subchapter explores the complexities of human relationships and the challenges of navigating the emotional landscape of isolation.

"I Can't Do This All by Myself: A Novel" captures the raw emotions and internal struggles of the protagonist as they come to terms with their own vulnerabilities and limitations. The subchapter "Feeling Out of Place" serves as a poignant reminder that we all long for connection and understanding, and that sometimes, the hardest part of being alone in a crowd is feeling like no one truly understands. Searching for a Connection

In the subchapter "Searching for a Connection" from the novel "Alone in a Crowd: A Novel of Isolation," the protagonist finds themselves grappling with feelings of loneliness and a sense of abandonment. As they navigate through their daily life, they can't shake the overwhelming sense of being alone in a crowded world.

The protagonist's inner dialogue echoes the sentiments of the audience, "I thought you would have been there for me." They long for a connection, for someone to understand their struggles and provide comfort in times of need. But as they reach out to those around them, they are met with indifference or shallow responses, leaving them feeling even more isolated.

The novel delves into the complexities of human relationships and the challenges of finding true connection in a world that often feels cold and uncaring. The protagonist's journey to find a meaningful connection resonates with readers who have experienced similar feelings of loneliness and longing for understanding.

Through the protagonist's struggles, the novel explores themes of self-reliance and the importance of reaching out for help when needed. The audience of "I Can't Do This All by My Self: A Novel" will find solace in the protagonist's journey and be reminded that they are not alone in their struggles.

As the protagonist continues to search for a connection, readers are taken on an emotional rollercoaster of highs and lows, ultimately leading to a deeper understanding of the human experience. The subchapter "Searching for a Connection" serves as a poignant reminder that we all crave connection and understanding, and that reaching out to others is a courageous act of vulnerability.

Chapter 2: The Mask

Pretending to Fit In

In the subchapter "Pretending to Fit In" from the novel "Alone in a Crowd: A Novel of Isolation," the protagonist finds themselves struggling to navigate the complexities of social interaction. As they observe others around them effortlessly blending in and forming connections, the feeling of isolation only intensifies. The pressure to conform and be accepted weighs heavily on their shoulders, leading them to put on a facade to fit in.

The protagonist finds themselves participating in activities they have no interest in, attending events they would rather avoid, and engaging in conversations that feel forced. They go to great lengths to Mold themselves into someone they believe others will accept, all the while feeling like an imposter in their own skin.

Despite their efforts to pretend, the protagonist can't shake the feeling of being alone in a crowd. They long for genuine connections and authentic relationships, but the fear of rejection holds them back. They struggle with feelings of inadequacy, questioning whether they will ever truly belong.

To the audience of "I thought you would have been there for me," this subchapter resonates deeply with those who have experienced the pain of feeling like an outsider. It speaks to the universal desire for acceptance and understanding, while also highlighting the internal battle that comes with pretending to be someone you're not.

In the niches of "I Can't Do This All by My Self: A Novel," readers will find solace in the protagonist's journey towards self-acceptance and the realization that true connection begins within. This subchapter serves as a reminder that it's okay to be different, to stand out, and to embrace the uniqueness that sets us apart from the crowd. Hiding True Feelings

"Hiding True Feelings" is a subchapter in the novel "Alone in a Crowd: A Novel of Isolation" that delves into the struggles of concealing one's true emotions from those around them. The protagonist grapples with the weight of their inner turmoil, feeling as though they are navigating the complexities of life alone.

Addressed to an audience of "I thought you would have been there for me," this subchapter explores the disappointment and betrayal that can come from feeling let down by those who are supposed to support us. The protagonist's journey of isolation and loneliness is exacerbated by the realization that even those closest to them may not truly understand or empathize with their inner struggles.

The niches of "I Can't Do This All by Myself: A Novel" are illuminated in this subchapter, as the protagonist grapples with the overwhelming burden of carrying their emotional burdens alone. The facade of strength and independence they present to the world begins to crack, revealing the vulnerability and pain that they have been hiding for so long.

As the protagonist navigates the complexities of their relationships and internal struggles, "Hiding True Feelings" serves as a poignant reminder of the power of vulnerability and authenticity. Through confronting their true emotions and seeking support from others, the protagonist begins to break free from the isolating grip of their own mind, finding solace and connection in the shared experiences of those around them. Longing for Authenticity

In the subchapter "Longing for Authenticity" of the novel "Alone in a Crowd," the protagonist grapples with the painful realization that the people they thought would always be there for them have let them down. The feeling of isolation and betrayal weighs heavily on their heart as they long for genuine connections and authenticity in their relationships.

The protagonist's journey towards self-discovery and understanding is a central theme in this subchapter. As they navigate through the complexities of human interactions, they come to realize the importance of being true to oneself and seeking out genuine connections with others. The longing for authenticity becomes a driving force in their quest for understanding and acceptance.

The audience of "I thought you would have been there for me" will resonate with the protagonist's struggles and emotions in this subchapter. The feeling of abandonment and disappointment is a universal experience that many can relate to, making this part of the novel particularly poignant and relatable.

For those in the niche of "I Can't Do This All by Myself: A Novel," this subchapter serves as a powerful reminder of the importance of reaching out for help and seeking genuine connections with others. The protagonist's journey towards self-acceptance and authenticity is a testament to the strength and resilience that can be found in vulnerability and openness.

Overall, "Longing for Authenticity" is a chapter that delves deep into the human experience of longing for connection and understanding in a world that often feels isolating and indifferent. Through the protagonist's journey, readers are reminded of the power of authenticity and genuine connections in overcoming feelings of loneliness and isolation.

Chapter 3: The Breaking Point

Walls Closing In

In the subchapter titled "Walls Closing In" from the novel "Alone in a Crowd: A Novel of Isolation," the protagonist finds themselves facing a deep sense of loneliness and abandonment. The feeling of being surrounded by walls that are slowly closing in on them becomes a metaphor for the isolation they are experiencing.

The protagonist reflects on the relationships they once had, particularly with someone they thought would always be there for them. The words "I thought you would have been there for me" echo in their mind, as they grapple with the realization that they are truly alone in their struggle.

As the walls continue to close in, the protagonist is forced to confront their own feelings of inadequacy and self-doubt. The familiar faces that once provided comfort now seem distant and unattainable, leaving them with a sense of helplessness and despair.

The subchapter delves into the complexities of human connection and the harsh reality that sometimes, we truly are alone in our struggles. The protagonist's journey through this emotional turmoil serves as a poignant reminder of the importance of reaching out for help and seeking support when we need it most.

For readers of "I Can't Do This All by Myself: A Novel," this subchapter will resonate deeply with themes of isolation and the fear of being left to face our demons alone. It serves as a powerful reminder of the strength we can find in vulnerability and the healing power of human connection. Reaching a Breaking Point

In the subchapter "Reaching a Breaking Point" of the novel "Alone in a Crowd," the protagonist finds themselves grappling with feelings of abandonment and isolation. The words "I thought you would have been there for me" echo in their mind, a haunting reminder of unmet expectations and shattered trust.

As the protagonist navigates the complexities of their relationships, they are forced to confront the harsh reality that they cannot rely on others to fulfil their emotional needs. The realization that they must face their struggles alone weighs heavily on their heart, leading to a sense of desolation and despair.

During their turmoil, the protagonist reaches a breaking point. The facade of strength and independence they have carefully constructed begins to crumble, revealing a vulnerable and wounded soul beneath. The pain of betrayal and disappointment threatens to consume them, leaving them feeling adrift in a sea of uncertainty and doubt.

As they struggle to make sense of their fractured relationships and unfulfilled expectations, the protagonist is forced to confront their own limitations and vulnerabilities. The journey towards self-acceptance and healing is a difficult and painful one, but ultimately necessary for their growth and resilience.

In the end, the protagonist learns that true strength comes from within, and that they can face their fears and overcoming their challenges with courage and grace. The subchapter "Reaching a Breaking Point" serves as a pivotal moment in their journey towards self-discovery and empowerment, as they come to understand that they are not alone in their struggles, but capable of finding solace and strength within themselves. Embracing Solitude

"Embracing Solitude"

To all those who have ever felt abandoned or let down by someone they thought would always be there for them, this subchapter is dedicated to you. It is a reminder that sometimes the only person we can truly rely on is ourselves. In the novel "Alone in a Crowd: A Novel of Isolation," the protagonist learns the hard way that placing all your trust in others can lead to disappointment and loneliness. But through this journey of self-discovery, he also comes to realize the power and beauty of embracing solitude.

"I thought you would have been there for me" is a sentiment that many of us can relate to. We have all experienced moments when we needed someone to lean on, only to find ourselves standing alone. It is in these moments of solitude that we are forced to confront our own fears and insecurities, but also discover our inner strength and resilience.

The novel "I Can't Do This All by My Self: A Novel" explores the theme of self-reliance and independence. The protagonist faces numerous challenges and setbacks, but ultimately learns that he can overcome them on his own. Through the process of embracing solitude, he finds a sense of freedom and empowerment that he never knew existed.

So, to all those who have ever felt abandoned or let down, remember that you are never truly alone. Embrace solitude as an opportunity for growth and self-discovery. Trust in yourself, believe in your own strength, and know that you can overcome any obstacle that comes your way. You are stronger than you think, and you have the power to create your own happiness and fulfilment.

Chapter 4: The Journey Within

Self-Reflection

Self-reflection is a powerful tool for personal growth and understanding. In times of isolation and feeling alone in a crowd, it can be especially important to take a step back and examine our thoughts, feelings, and actions. This process can help us gain insight into our own behaviours and emotions, as well as how they may be impacting our relationships with others.

"I thought you would have been there for me" is a common sentiment expressed by those who feel let down by someone they expected support from. In these moments, it can be easy to blame others for our feelings of isolation and loneliness. However, self-reflection allows us to look inward and consider our own role in these situations. Are there ways in which we may have contributed to the breakdown of a relationship or the feeling of being alone in a crowd?

In the novel "Alone in a Crowd: A Novel of Isolation," the protagonist grapples with these questions as she navigates through feelings of loneliness and isolation. Through self-reflection, he begins to uncover deeper truths about his self and his relationships with others. This process of introspection leads him to a greater sense of self-awareness and a deeper understanding of his own needs and desires.

For those who resonate with the niche of "I Can't Do This All by My Self: A Novel," self-reflection can be a powerful tool for navigating through feelings of isolation and loneliness. By taking the time to look inward and examine our own thoughts and emotions, we can begin to heal from past hurts and build stronger, more fulfilling connections with those around us.
Discovering Strength

In the subchapter "Discovering Strength" of the novel "Alone in a Crowd: A Novel of Isolation," the protagonist finds themselves facing a difficult reality: the person they thought would always be there for them has let them down. The feeling of betrayal and abandonment is overwhelming, leaving them feeling truly alone in a crowded world.

As the protagonist navigates this new sense of isolation, they begin to realize that relying solely on others for support and validation is not sustainable. They must dig deep within themselves to find the strength to carry on, even when it feels like the world is against them.

Through moments of self-reflection and introspection, the protagonist starts to discover a resilience they never knew they had. They come to understand that they are capable of overcoming challenges and hardships on their own, without needing constant reassurance from others.

This realization marks a pivotal moment in the protagonist's journey towards self-discovery and personal growth. They learn that true strength comes from within, and that they are more powerful than they ever imagined.

To the audience of "I thought you would have been there for me," this subchapter serves as a powerful reminder that we cannot always rely on others to be our pillars of support.

Sometimes, we must find the strength within ourselves to keep moving forward, even when it feels like the world is against us.

For readers of the niche novel "I Can't Do This All by My Self: A Novel," this subchapter speaks to the universal struggle of feeling alone in a crowded world and the ultimate realization that we are stronger than we think. It is a testament to the power of resilience and self-reliance in the face of adversity. Embracing Independence

In the subchapter "Embracing Independence" of "Alone in a Crowd: A Novel of Isolation," the protagonist finally comes to terms with the fact that they cannot rely on others to provide them with the support and validation they need. As they navigate through their feelings of abandonment and disappointment, they begin to realize that true independence comes from within.

Addressed to an audience of "I thought you would have been there for me," this subchapter delves into the complexities of expecting others to fulfil our needs and the harsh reality that sometimes, we must learn to stand on our own two feet. The protagonist's journey towards self-reliance is a poignant reminder that we are ultimately responsible for our own happiness and well-being.

For readers of "I Can't Do This All by Myself: A Novel," this subchapter serves as a powerful exploration of the struggles and triumphs that come with embracing independence. It challenges the notion that we need someone else to complete us and instead encourages us to find fulfilment and strength from within.

As the protagonist grapples with their newfound sense of self-reliance, they begin to understand that true independence is not about shutting others out, but rather about recognizing our own worth and capabilities. They learn that while it may be lonely at times, the freedom and empowerment that come from embracing independence are invaluable.

"Embracing Independence" is a crucial turning point in the protagonist's journey towards self-discovery and acceptance. It is a reminder to all readers that while it may be daunting to walk the path alone, true growth and fulfilment can only be achieved when we learn to rely on ourselves.

Chapter 5: The Revelation

Realizing Inner Worth

To the audience of "I thought you would have been there for me" and the niches of "I Can't Do This All by My Self: A Novel," this subchapter focuses on the journey of self-discovery and self-worth. In a world where we often seek validation and acceptance from others, it is crucial to remember that our true worth comes from within.

Throughout the novel "Alone in a Crowd: A Novel of Isolation," the protagonist faces challenges that force them to confront their inner demons and insecurities. It is only through this journey that they begin to realize their own value and worth, independent of the opinions of others.

Realizing inner worth is a transformative process that requires self-reflection, self-compassion, and self-acceptance. It is about recognizing that your worth does not depend on external factors or validation from others. You are enough just as you are, and your worth is inherent and undeniable.

As you navigate through the pages of this novel, remember that your worth is not defined by your past mistakes, your failures, or the opinions of others. It is about embracing your unique qualities, strengths, and potential. It is about recognizing your own value and treating yourself with kindness and respect.

So, to the reader who feels alone and isolated, remember that you are not defined by your circumstances. You have the power to redefine your own worth and create a life filled with meaning, purpose, and self-love. Embrace the journey of self-discovery and realize that you are worthy of all the love and happiness that life has to offer. Finding Peace in Solitude

To the audience of "I thought you would have been there for me," this subchapter on "Finding Peace in Solitude" delves into the importance of learning to be comfortable in our own company, even when we feel let down by others. In the novel "Alone in a Crowd: A Novel of Isolation," the protagonist grapples with feelings of abandonment and disappointment from those they expected to be there for them. However, through their journey of self-discovery, they come to realize that true peace and solace can be found within themselves.

In a world that often feels crowded with expectations and demands, it can be easy to lose sight of the value of solitude. But in moments of solitude, we can reconnect with ourselves, to reflect on our own needs and desires, and to find a sense of inner peace that can sustain us through even the most challenging times.

"I Can't Do This All by My Self: A Novel" explores the theme of self-reliance and the power that comes from learning to stand on our own two feet. While it may be painful to feel let down by others, it is also an opportunity to cultivate a deeper sense of self-awareness and resilience. By finding peace in solitude, we can learn to rely on ourselves for comfort and strength, rather than seeking validation or support from external sources.

Ultimately, the journey to finding peace in solitude is a deeply personal one. It requires us to confront our fears and insecurities, to embrace our vulnerabilities, and to cultivate a sense of self-love and acceptance. But in doing so, we can discover a newfound sense of freedom and empowerment that allows us to navigate the challenges of life with grace and resilience. Embracing Being Alone in a Crowd

In the subchapter "Embracing Being Alone in a Crowd" from "Alone in a Crowd: A Novel of Isolation," we delve into the complex emotions that come with feeling alone even during a bustling crowd. The protagonist grapples with the realization that despite being surrounded by people, they still feel a profound sense of isolation. This struggle is something that many of us can relate to, as we navigate the ups and downs of our own relationships and connections.

For those who have experienced the feeling of being let down by someone they thought would always be there for them, the notion of embracing solitude in a crowd can be both comforting and unsettling. It forces us to confront our own inner strength and resilience, even when faced with disappointment and betrayal.

"I Can't Do This All by My Self: A Novel" speaks to the inherent human desire for companionship and support, but also acknowledges the power that can come from learning to rely on oneself. The protagonist learns to find solace in their own company, realizing that they are capable of weathering the storms of life without always needing someone else by their side.

As we journey with the protagonist through their struggles and triumphs, we are reminded of the importance of self-reliance and inner strength. Embracing being alone in a crowd is not about shutting oneself off from the world, but rather about finding peace and contentment within one's own being. It is a powerful reminder that we are never truly alone if we have the courage to embrace ourselves and our own unique journey.

Chapter 6: The New Beginning

Embracing Individuality

Embracing individuality is a crucial theme in the novel "Alone in a Crowd: A Novel of Isolation." The protagonist, struggling with feelings of loneliness and isolation, must learn to embrace their own unique identity to find peace and fulfilment. This subchapter delves into the importance of self-acceptance and the power of embracing one's individuality.

In a world where we are constantly bombarded with images of perfection and pressure to conform, it can be easy to lose sight of who we truly are. The protagonist's journey towards self-discovery is a powerful reminder that we must embrace our differences and quirks to truly thrive. By celebrating what makes us unique, we can find a sense of belonging and connection that goes beyond superficial expectations.

The subchapter "Embracing Individuality" challenges the audience of "I thought you would have been there for me" to reflect on their own identities and the ways in which they may be hiding or suppressing their true selves. It encourages readers to embrace their flaws and imperfections as part of what makes them special and worthy of love.

Through the protagonist's struggles and triumphs, readers are reminded that true happiness comes from within and that by embracing our individuality, we can find the strength to overcome even the deepest feelings of isolation. "Alone in a Crowd" serves as a powerful reminder that we are all worthy of love and acceptance, just as we are. Building a Support System

In the subchapter "Building a Support System" of the novel "Alone in a Crowd: A Novel of Isolation," the protagonist finds themselves grappling with the realization that they cannot navigate life's challenges alone. The words "I thought you would have been there for me" echo in their mind, highlighting the disappointment and sense of abandonment they feel from their perceived support system.

As the protagonist comes to terms with the harsh reality of their situation, they begin to understand the importance of building a strong support system. They realize that relying solely on one person for emotional or mental support is not sustainable and can lead to feelings of isolation and despair.

The subchapter delves into the protagonist's journey of seeking out new connections and fostering existing relationships that can provide the support and understanding they need. They learn to lean on friends, family, or even professional resources to help them navigate the challenges they face.

Through this process, the protagonist discovers the power of vulnerability and reaching out for help when needed. They come to understand that it is okay to admit when they are struggling and to ask for support from those around them.

"Building a Support System" serves as a pivotal moment in the novel, as the protagonist learns to let go of their pride and self-reliance in Favor of building a network of people who can offer them the support and guidance they need to thrive. This subchapter speaks to the universal truth that we all need a support system to lean on during life's trials and tribulations. Thriving in Isolation

To the audience feeling abandoned and alone, the subchapter "Thriving in Isolation" offers a glimmer of hope and empowerment. In the novel "Alone in a Crowd," the protagonist discovers the strength within themselves to not only survive but thrive in isolation. This subchapter serves as a reminder that even in the darkest of times, there is a light at the end of the tunnel.

The journey of thriving in isolation begins with self-reflection and acceptance. The protagonist learns to embrace their own company and finds solace in solitude. By turning inward and exploring their thoughts and emotions, they uncover a newfound sense of self-awareness and inner peace.

As the protagonist navigates the challenges of isolation, they discover hidden talents and passions that were previously overlooked. They find joy in simple pleasures and learn to appreciate the beauty of the world around them. Through this process of self-discovery, they come to realize that they are capable of so much more than they ever thought possible.

The subchapter "Thriving in Isolation" is a reminder that even when it feels like the world has turned its back on us, we have the power to create our own happiness and fulfilment. It is a testament to the resilience of the human spirit and the ability to find strength in the face of adversity.

So, to the audience feeling abandoned and alone, remember that you are not defined by the presence or absence of others in your life. You have the power to thrive in isolation and emerge stronger and more resilient than ever before. Embrace the journey of self-discovery and know that you can overcome any obstacle that comes your way.

Chapter 7: The Epiphany

Understanding the Power of Solitude

In the subchapter "Understanding the Power of Solitude" from the novel "Alone in a Crowd: A Novel of Isolation," the author delves into the concept of being alone and the importance of solitude in one's life. To the audience of "I thought you would have been there for me," this subchapter offers a different perspective on the idea of isolation and how it can be empowering.

The author explores the notion that being alone does not necessarily equate to loneliness. Solitude can be a time for self-reflection, self-discovery, and personal growth. It allows individuals to reconnect with themselves and gain a better understanding of their own thoughts and feelings.

In a world where we are constantly surrounded by noise and distractions, the power of solitude lies in its ability to provide a sense of peace and clarity. It allows us to tune out the external influences and focus on our own inner voice. This can be incredibly liberating and empowering, as it enables us to make decisions based on our own values and desires rather than being swayed by the opinions of others.

For those in the niche of "I Can't Do This All by Myself: A Novel," this subchapter serves as a reminder that while it may feel daunting to be alone, there is strength to be found in solitude. It is a time to recharge, regroup, and rediscover oneself. By embracing the power of solitude, individuals can learn to rely on themselves and cultivate a sense of independence and self-reliance.

Ultimately, "Understanding the Power of Solitude" challenges the notion that being alone is a negative experience. Instead, it encourages readers to embrace solitude as a valuable opportunity for personal growth and introspection. Finding Joy in Being Alone

In the subchapter "Finding Joy in Being Alone" from the book "Alone in a Crowd: A Novel of Isolation," the protagonist explores the concept of solitude as a source of empowerment and self-discovery. As the character navigates the challenges of being alone in a crowded world, they come to realize the beauty and freedom that can be found in solitude.

The protagonist learns that being alone does not have to equate to loneliness or isolation. In fact, it can be a time for self-reflection, personal growth, and inner peace. By embracing solitude, the character discovers a newfound sense of independence and self-reliance. They learn to appreciate their own company and find joy in the simple moments of quiet reflection.

Through moments of solitude, the character begins to understand themselves better and gain a deeper appreciation for their own strengths and capabilities. They realize that they can find happiness and fulfilment within themselves, rather than relying on others for validation or companionship.

The subchapter "Finding Joy in Being Alone" serves as a reminder to the audience of "I thought you would have been there for me" that true happiness comes from within. It encourages readers to embrace moments of solitude as opportunities for self-discovery and personal growth. By learning to find joy in being alone, the protagonist sets an example for others struggling with feelings of loneliness or isolation.

For fans of the niche "I Can't Do This All by My Self: A Novel," this subchapter offers a poignant exploration of the power of solitude and self-reliance. It reminds readers that they can find happiness and fulfilment on their own, without needing validation or support from others. Ultimately, "Finding Joy in Being Alone" is a celebration of the strength and resilience that can be found within each of us when we embrace the beauty of solitude. Embracing the Journey of Self-Discovery

In the subchapter "Embracing the Journey of Self-Discovery" from "Alone in a Crowd: A Novel of Isolation," we delve into the complex and transformative process of understanding oneself. Oftentimes, we may find ourselves feeling alone and abandoned, wondering why those we thought would be there for us have seemingly disappeared. It is in these moments of solitude that we are forced to confront our true selves and embark on a journey of self-discovery.

The protagonist of our story grapples with feelings of isolation and abandonment, questioning why they have been left to navigate this challenging journey alone. However, as they begin to delve deeper into their own thoughts and emotions, they realize that true strength comes from within. By embracing the journey of self-discovery, they uncover hidden depths of resilience and courage that they never knew existed.

"I Can't Do This All by My Self: A Novel" speaks to the universal experience of feeling lost and alone, but ultimately finding solace and empowerment in the process of self-discovery. Through introspection and self-reflection, the protagonist learns to lean into their own inner strength and embrace the journey ahead with newfound confidence.

To the audience of "I thought you would have been there for me," this subchapter serves as a reminder that true companionship begins with oneself. By embracing the journey of self-discovery, we can learn to rely on our own inner resources and find a sense of peace and fulfilment that no external validation can provide. Embracing solitude as an opportunity for growth and self-awareness, we can emerge stronger and more resilient than ever before.

Chapter 8: The Transformation

Embracing Isolation as a Strength

In the subchapter "Embracing Isolation as a Strength" of the novel "Alone in a Crowd," the protagonist grapples with the feelings of abandonment and loneliness that often come with isolation. The protagonist, speaking to the audience of "I thought you would have been there for me," reflects on the ways in which they have felt let down by those they once relied on for support.

As the protagonist navigates their solitude, they begin to see isolation not as a weakness, but as a source of inner strength. They realize that being alone does not mean being weak or incapable, but rather offers them the opportunity to tap into their own resilience and self-reliance. Through moments of introspection and self-discovery, the protagonist learns to embrace their isolation as a chance to grow and thrive on their own terms.

The subchapter delves into the protagonist's journey towards self-acceptance and empowerment, showing how they come to understand that they do not need others to validate their worth or happiness. Instead, they find solace in their own company and discover a newfound sense of independence and confidence.

For readers who resonate with the themes of loneliness and self-sufficiency, "Alone in a Crowd" offers a poignant exploration of the ways in which isolation can be reframed as a source of strength rather than weakness. Through the protagonist's experiences, readers are encouraged to embrace their own solitude and find the inner resources to navigate life's challenges with grace and resilience. Living Authentically

In the subchapter "Living Authentically" from the novel "Alone in a Crowd: A Novel of Isolation," the protagonist grapples with the idea of being true to oneself in a world that often demands conformity. The protagonist, feeling isolated and abandoned by those they thought would always be there, embarks on a journey of self-discovery and introspection.

As the protagonist navigates the challenges of loneliness and alienation, they come to realize the importance of living authentically. They learn that true fulfilment can only be found by embracing their unique identity and staying true to their values and beliefs, even when it may be difficult or unpopular.

Throughout the subchapter, the protagonist confronts their fears and insecurities, ultimately finding the strength to break free from the expectations of others and chart their own course. They discover that true happiness and inner peace can only be achieved by being true to oneself and living in alignment with one's true desires and aspirations.

The subchapter "Living Authentically" serves as a powerful reminder to the audience of "I thought you would have been there for me" that true connection and fulfilment can only be found by embracing one's authentic self. It encourages readers to break free from the constraints of societal expectations and to embrace their uniqueness and individuality.

For those in the niche of "I Can't Do This All by My Self: A Novel," this subchapter offers a message of hope and empowerment. It reminds readers that they have the strength and resilience to overcome challenges and find their way back to themselves, even in the face of loneliness and isolation. Ultimately, "Living Authentically" serves as a beacon of light for

those who may feel lost or alone, offering a path towards self-discovery and inner peace.
Finding Fulfilment in Being Alone in a Crowd

In a world where we are constantly surrounded by people, finding fulfilment in being alone in a crowd can seem like a daunting task. But the truth is, there is beauty in solitude and strength in being able to stand alone, even during a bustling crowd.

For those who have ever felt the sting of betrayal or abandonment, the idea of finding peace and contentment in solitude may seem impossible. The feeling of being left alone when you thought someone would be there for you can be incredibly painful. But what if we shifted our perspective and saw being alone as an opportunity for growth and self-discovery?

In the novel "Alone in a Crowd: A Novel of Isolation," the protagonist grapples with the harsh reality of being let down by those she thought she could rely on. As she navigates the complexities of isolation, she discovers that true fulfilment can be found in the moments of solitude and self-reflection.

Being alone in a crowd doesn't have to be a negative experience. It can be a time for introspection, creativity, and personal growth. By embracing your own company and finding peace within yourself, you can learn to rely on your own strength and resilience.

So, to those who feel like they can't do it all by themselves, remember that being alone is not a weakness, but a strength. It is an opportunity to connect with yourself on a deeper level and find fulfilment in your own company. Embrace the solitude, and you may just find that you are stronger and more resilient than you ever thought possible.